A modern Bard's book of poem's

Gary Macgregor

BookLeaf Publishing

India | USA | UK

Presentation by *BookLeaf Publishing*

Web: www.bookleafpub.com

E-mail: info@bookleafpub.com

ISBN: 9789360949969

First edition 2024

*To my wife and children and the mysteries of
the Akashic record.*

ACKNOWLEDGEMENT

Bookleaf Publishing for a wonderful opportunity and challenge!
My wife Alison, the inspiration for so many poems when we were young.

PREFACE

Gary the Bard, a Sussex poet from Scotland has found inspiration for his short poems from a wide variety of sources and experience. From teenage love and longing to the tragic loss of his mother to his Harley Davidson and anything else that moves him. this is an eclectic group of short poems that I hope you enjoy!

The Wolf and the Hart

A snowy white Hart
Was chased by the pack
Into a Glen made of stone
With nowhere to run
And nowhere to hide
They soon would reduce her to bone

"Please wait my lord wolf,
And please do not bite,
You may find I have something to say.
You've cornered me here
The game is well won,
But you can only eat me today"

"What will you do my lord wolf
When all deer are gone?
And nothing is left for your bite
You are the lords
And we are the prey
But listen and you may find I'm right"

"Your help my lord wolf
I may need it now
For the herd have all gone astray
All overgrown

The forest will be
When the deer have all gone away"

"So how will you hunt
And how will you see
With the forest no longer kept clear?
Can you live my lord wolf
And will you survive
If you eat all the beautiful deer"

"Make a pact my lord wolf
To look after the herd
To keep it all healthy and strong
Wise words, my lord wolf
I wait on thee here
To see if my counsel is wrong"

"Brave are you my Hart
When surrounded in fear
To speak up for your herd and your kin
All lives are in balance
I see it now clear
The herd already is getting too thin"

"Wise words you speak
Oh snowy white Hart,
But the wolves must still make a kill
So look after the forests
We'll manage the Herd

And take only the old or the ill"

"Go now, my young Hart
And carry this news
You now may leave without fear
Return to your Herd
And sleep well tonight
You have till the end of the year"

"Thank you, my lord wolf
I will take your leave
Off into the forest I'll go"
The Snowy White Hart
Then bounded away
And vanished in the White Snow.

Nonsense

I wrote wise words
And made them rhyme
To tell a story
Out of time

But of these words
I must confess
I had no time
No more, no less.

The High Weald of Sussex

5

From the Southdowns, to the High Weald
Walking through forest, stream, track and field
Finding Bilberries, Currants, Ransoms and more
New woodlands and rivers for me to explore
With no footpaths, I wander away from the track
With basket in hand and bent over back
I pluck a small berry, a feast for a king
Gathering food for free is my favourite thing
Settling down by the fire to make me a meal
Taking no more than you need is always the deal
A full belly and warmth at the end of the day
Is all a man needs, I wish I could stay
But as the fire burns low and the shadows they
creep
I dream of mountains and forests and drift off to
sleep

A Christmas I Remember

A Christmas I remember,
When Christmases were white
A Christmas I remember,
Getting up when its still night

A noise would wake me
I would catch a little flash of red
I rubbed the sleep out of my eyes
And tip toed out of bed

Still half asleep, I thought I saw
A little something white
Was it his beard, or snow outside
Or was it just the light?

Creeping gently down the stairs
To see if He had been
The mince pie gone, the whiskey drunk
But He was barely seen

No trace downstairs, that I can see
And not the smallest sound
Until I spy a note above
A footprint on the ground

"Off to bed, my little one
A secret I shall let
If you look for me or dont believe
No pressie shall you get!"

I scurried quick, back to my room
And straight into my bed
I believe in Santa Claus
And every word he said

A Christmas I remember
So long now it must seem
The night I almost saw him
Or was it just a dream....

Away Hame to Alba

I'm away off to Alba
Takin' the long road back hame
Dreaming of time gone by
But the worlds no longer the same

I struggle to find my way
In the streets I thought I knew
There are no familiar faces
In this unfamiliar view

Can I really call this home
Three decades I've been gone
A lifetime since I lived here
Maybe its just been too long

And yet this land begat me
still it calls me home
It draws me ever Northwards
Whichever way I roam

And so i'll slowly wander
From the mountains to the sea
I'll let the winds take me
To where i'm meant to be

I Wish

I wish things were not as they are
I wish we could still chat, as we sit in the car
I wish we could still hug and cuddle and kiss
I wish you were with me for its us that I miss

I wish I wasn't alone of a night
I wish I could see you 'fore I turn out the light
I wish you would whisper "don't go to sleep yet"
I wish things were as they were when we met

I wish each of us were single as we have been
before
Then I'd wish just to see you and be alone no
more
And with each time I wished, if something came
true
Then for now you'd be single until I found you

But my day will be empty, I'll have no meal and
no wine
I'll be alone in our room, with no valentine.

The Archer

A Bow is Yew so thin and strong
Almost broken at six foot long
As I carve and sand and scrape
From twig to bow it now takes shape
In my minds eye I start to see
The yew bow now is part of me

The bow I shape its nearly gone
The wood left now cant last that long
The stick I carve so nearly broken
All that's left so mere a token
Its wood is hart to draw so deep
Its wood is sap your hand to keep

Its arrows sent to fly so high
Then rain like thunder from the sky
We send it high to find its way
Into the sky were dead men lay
It finds its mark your broken too
Just like the bow that sent for you

Your bow a tender agile stick
So strong a pull released so quick
My bow is keen my arrow fast
Ninth tenths gone we save the last

A Bow is man when sleek and strong
But so short lived so fleet and gone

A life of toil, hurts unhealed
So much loss this life I yield
Almost broken yet almost true
Did you not see the bow is you

Bonnie Scotland

In the lands of hill and glen
I was born now long ago
And though i'm very far from home
I'm marching North to meet the snow

In the land where red deer run
On Rocky shore or beech of sand
In woods that seldom see the sun
To home to home to our Scotland

The pines grow tall, the squirrel red
The mountains large and steep
The heather soft for weary head
To send you off to sleep

Rough is this land that hardens you
It tests both will and might
But on and on we all must go
We'll march on through the night

Its time to rest my weary feet
The sunrise brings the light
For one more day I must endure
Alas Scotland's in sight.

Half a hundred men

Give me half a hundred men my lord
And I shall turn the tide
Give me archers and some scouts
And I'll take these men out wide

With half a hundred men, my lord
I'll fight through to the king
His head delivered to your feet
His crown to you I'll bring

We'll go by stealth and cunning low
We'll creep out this very night
Amongst the shadows and the tree's
Until your crown's insight

First to the North and then the West
We'll come around their flank
We'll silence sentries and their scouts
Then creep along the bank

By the time the sun is risen
And the minstrels start to sing
With half a hundred men, my lord
By 'morrow you'll be king!

Auld Years Night

Its Auld years night
Another year gone by
Its time to remember friends of old
As the tears brim at my eye

For I have loved and lost
Both family and friends
And yet I linger, waiting here
i'm yet to see all ends

I remember such good times
with shared memories in kind
my friends you maybe out of sight
but your never out of mind

How I long to sit beside you
Pour a wee dram on your grave
Chat like you can hear me
And give thanks for all you gave

My Mum must be Galadriel

My Mum must be Galadriel.
A secret kept, I cannot tell,
For no-one must ever know
Even I'm not sure, can it be so?

I swear she did, when I was small,
She wove a spell so I'd grow tall.
Like Elven folk be brave and fair,
With her green eyes and golden hair.

My Mothers magic, plain to see
Came from her kitchen, her bakery,
Macaroon and tablet and millionaires,
Meringues with butter icing layers.

A passion she had for reading too:
The Hobbit and Dune to name a few,
And in these book's I saw her name
The lady of light we call Elaine.

A woman who would dance and play,
A wife at night, but mum by day,
Five children she had and lots of fun,
Twice a daughter and thrice a son.

A life on Earth does wax and wane,
As summer fades to winter again.
But to live forever, as Elven folk do,
Needs only love, from me to you.

So many thoughts, to have and hold,
Many tales, and stories told,
But I have one last word, last tale to tell
I know my Mum is Galadriel!

The Dark Shadow of Death

The dark shadow of death
Will come for us all
I expect him, I am waiting
I rejoice in your call

To take me away
Now what a relief
My days here are done
Still you come like a thief

No need to sneak up
I am not unawares
I knew you were coming
I've taken my cares

My affairs are in order
I'm ready to leave
But where will you take me
With my hand on your sleeve

And what will you show me
What good have I done
Or will you revel in mischief
And spoil my fun

All before me have gone
Now I am the last
Life flashes before me
Who'll remember my past

Am I forgotten
As life slowly roll's on
Time so relentless
Now everyone gone

This world is now over
All is extinct
consumed by our star
We've gone to the brink

Lucky Number

What's for you won't go by you
My mother said of old
You wont miss out on your fate
And that's what I've been told

The more you try to swerve away
The more you try to run
A self-fulfilling prophecy
Is all that you've begun

So don't fret what's round the corner
'Cos if you try to flee
You'll run into the arms of fate
Just where your meant to be

For my Sweethart

The wind blows upon the flag
And ripples with the moon
A sudden realistation comes
to know we parted all too soon

The stars sparkle with the night
And the sun calls up the day
To know my grief began
when you kissed me and walked away

My love is like a star
That sparkles in the night
And like the sky, I feel blue
When you're out of sight

The thought that keeps me going
Is that we'll be together soon
And knowing that we're both under
The same old stars and moon

Young Love

When love is around
you'll know it's there
you see the girl
with long red hair

She'll turn around
And look at you
When love is there
What can you do

You have that feeling
In your heart
When love is around
And about to start

She looks at you
With big brown eyes
your legs tremble
Then paralyse

She smiles at you
Then turns away
Love is here
And here to stay

Love will come
And when it's true
I'll know the one I love
Is you!

For Nana

She said, its time, I need to go
Been here too long, I need to know

What lays beyond the vale of Death
I'm ready now, just one last breath

Remember me, I'm Jeannie Doo
Remember all I did for you

As I grow weak, I'm nearly done
Tell Charlie Boy, my only son

So write these words and be my Bard
For I'm off now, to the knackers yard.

Oh Ma Wee Darlin'

Written for my Dad for his "Wee Darlin"

Oh ma wee Darlin'
Ma wee December Rose
Your smile was like all the flowers in a meadow
And ma love for you still grows

Oh ma wee Darlin'
I'll miss you forever more
You filled up all my sense and being
Your loss has cut me to the core

Oh ma wee Darlin'
How can I go on?
Without you to walk beside me
I can't believe your gone

Oh ma wee Darlin'
I'll love you everyday
I'll talk and chat and laugh and shout
As if you'd never gone away

Oh ma wee Darlin'
I know we'll meet again
So watch me from the stars above
And I'll see you at the end.

Love

The days are bright
But lonely
The skies are clear
But blue
My world is complete
But empty
And I am whole but half
Without you

A Moment Gone

I wondered why you held me tight
I wondered why you cried
I saw your heart was breaking
It was then I knew I'd died

I know you cannot see me
And now I cannot touch
I'm sitting here beside you
I still need you oh so much

So think of me living
As I am in your heart
Think of me with you
We're never far apart

I see you when you laugh
I'm with you when you cry
How I want to hold you
I never meant to die

Think of me often
I'm never far away
I am watching over you
Beside you I will stay

I see a light is calling me
I feel its gentle draw
But I know I cannot leave you
The pain is still too raw

The light is getting stronger
It pulls on me to leave
I linger on beside you
To help you as you grieve

I feel an overwhelming love
I know I cannot stay
"I'll love you forever"
Is the last I hear you say

You held me as I fell asleep
You heard my last deep sigh
You know I'll love you always
I never meant to die.

Guard Duty

I'm smoking spliffs
I'm taking E
So let me out
I want to be free
I'm a sweaty old driver
Old songs I've sung
So I want to get out
To live while I'm young
I want to get pissed
Take drugs and shag
And fuck off the days
With a post coital fag
And then when I'm free
And the old days are gone
I'll come back to the gate
And say "fucking stag on."

Harley Davidson Iron 883

28 Degrees of lean
100 degrees of mean
As I tear through the streets
On my Harley Davidson
Dark custom wrecking machine

To the seat, to the bar
To the breaks, I'm out my car
I'm on my bikes two wheels
I'm gonna go far

I've got the road, it opens up
I've got the wind in my hair
I'm leaving life behind,
Like I don't fucking care

Got the freedom, got the pace
Got the miles, got the space
On my Harley, on the road
Gotta win life's race

Got the throttle, got the fuel
Ride the bends feel the pull
Faster and faster
Its my number one rule

Now everything's a blur
Everything is one
I can't catch the light
Though I'm chasing the sun

Tearing through the night
Like a shadow
Can't be seen
Bending the bike to
28 degrees of lean.